ISBN: 978-0-9988220-0-6

First Edition

Find activities related to zoo animals at
pinterest.com/loisbaron600/boards

Backsides: Zoo Animals

Lois M. Baron

All-Around Publishing ~ Arlington, Virginia

Rhinoceros

Polar Bear

Elephant & Calf

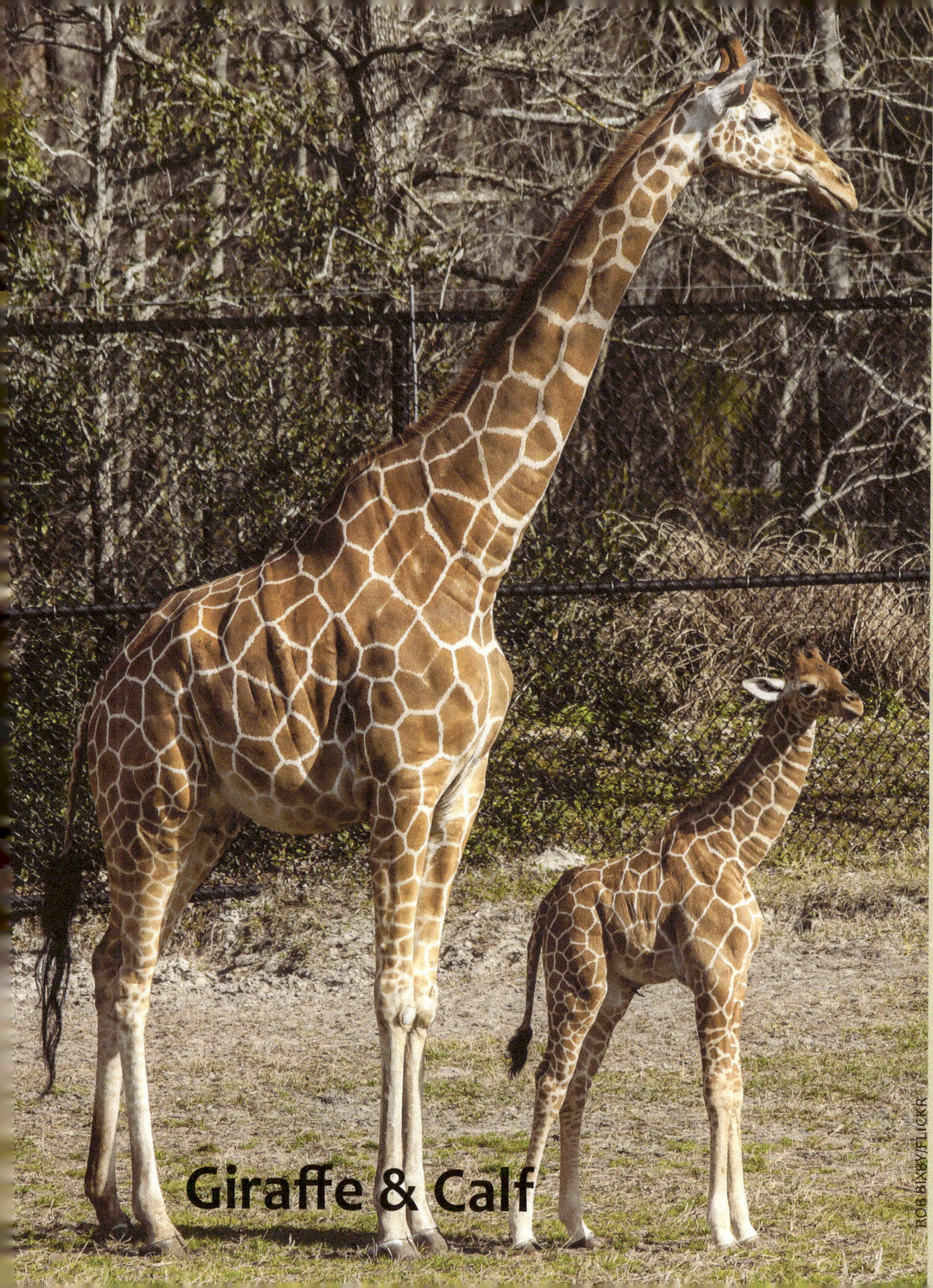

Giraffe & Calf

Koala

Tiger

Peacock

Orangutan

Zebra

Penguin

Camel

Hippopotamus & Calf

Fun Facts about These Animals

Camel
Camels live about 40 years. They can eat thorns. They can go 10 months without drinking. Baby camels are born without humps. Humps contain fat, not water.

Elephant
An elephant's nose has 16 muscles. Its trunk has more than 100,000 muscles. African savanna elephants have large ears shaped much like the continent of Africa. African forest elephants have large oval ears. Asian elephants have small ears.

Giraffe
The tallest giraffes can be taller than a double-decker bus. They have the same number of bones in their neck as humans. A giraffe heart is the biggest of any land mammal.

Hippopotamus
A hippo's lower teeth may get long-er than 12 inches. Hippos can hold their breath for five minutes under water. A calf is born weighing an average of 99 pounds.

Koala
Koalas are like kangeroos—they carry their babies in a pouch for six or seven months. Babies are called joeys. Koalas live in Australia.

Orangutan
Orangutans like to be alone. They are the largest mammals that live in trees, even though the biggest ones can weigh 300 pounds. They are the only great apes that live in Asia.

Peacock
A peacock is what a boy peafowl is called. A family of peafowl is known as a bevy. Peacocks shed their beautiful feathers each year. They can fly.

Penguin
Seventeen kinds of penguins live in the Southern Hemisphere. They range from 14 inches high to 45 inches high, on average. Emperor penguins can stay underwater for around 20 minutes at a time. Penguins sneeze to get rid of the seawater they ingest while hunting for fish.

Polar Bear
Polar bears have uneven skin on the soles of the feet, which helps to prevent slipping. In swimming the polar bear uses only its front limbs. Its tail is 3–5 inches long.

Rhinoceros
Rhinoceroses see badly, but smell and hear very well. Rhino skin can be as much as 2 inches thick.

Tiger
Tigers like to eat porcupines. Cubs are born blind, and it can take up to two months for them to see clearly. Tigers like to swim.

Zebra
Each zebra's stripes are slightly different from every other zebra's. Underneath their stripes is black skin. They look like horses but hate to be ridden. A group of zebras is called a zeal.

pinterest.com/loisbaron600

facebook.com/LoisBaron.Author

twitter.com/backsidesbooks